Contents

Chapter 1
Introducing Publisher

What is Microsoft Publisher?

Microsoft Publisher is a high-powered desktop publishing program. Its uses range from creating simple party invitations to more complex applications such as professional-looking newspapers and even books!

This chapter is designed to ease you into the basics of the package and its look and feel. You will start off by creating the structure of a basic publication using a template which will then be personalised in Chapter 2.

Getting Started

▶ Load Microsoft Publisher. This can be done in either of two ways:

▶ You can double-click the Publisher icon

Microsoft Publisher

▶ Or click Start at the bottom left of the screen, then click Programs, then the Microsoft Publisher option.

▶ Your screen will look like the one on the page opposite:

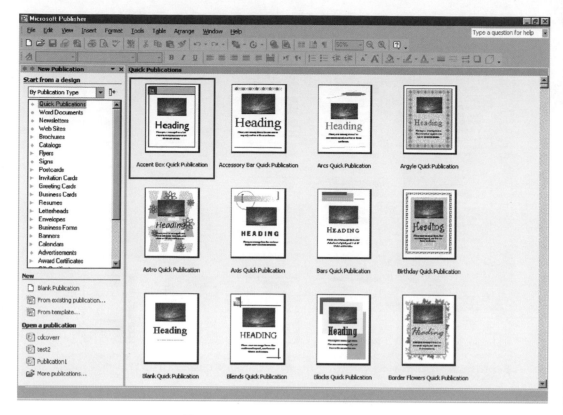

Figure 1.1: The opening screen

Using the Task pane

The Task pane is the easiest way to produce a publication because it does all the work for you. All you need to do is to select options in the Task pane and away it goes.

In this chapter you are going to use it to produce a simple leaflet advertising a school disco.

> In the Task pane (on the left of the screen), make sure By Publication Type is selected.

> Select Flyers in the list of designs and click on Announcement when it expands.

> Click the Party Announcement Flyer.

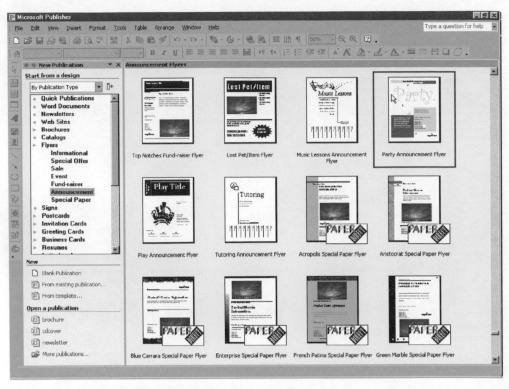

Figure 1.2: Starting the Party Announcement Flyer

The flyer is loaded into Publisher and you can now edit how the leaflet will look.

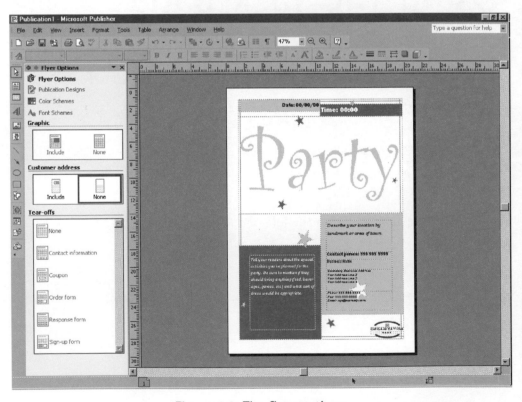

Figure 1.3: The flyer options

Choosing a colour scheme

Now you need to select a colour scheme for your flyer. It is a good idea to choose something bright that will grab everybody's attention when they see it.

 Click Colour Schemes in the Task pane.

 Select the Citrus color scheme.

Amending Personal Details

 Click Edit on the main menu bar.

 Click Personal Information.

If you know that your details are already correct you can skip forward to the next section, The Party Flyer.

Note:
You will only need to fill in your personal information details once because Publisher remembers them for next time you load it up

Terry showed the gang you're never too young to do the Funky Chicken - "Bongo style"!

Next you will see the Personal Information window. If you want the details to appear as in this tutorial, fill in the details like those shown in the screen below:

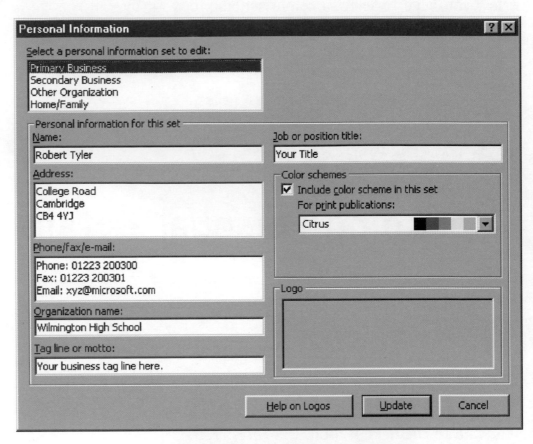

Figure 1.4: Updating your Personal Information

 Click in the box to **Include color scheme** in this set.

 Click **Update**.

The Party Flyer

Your flyer should now look like this:

Figure 1.5: Your party flyer

To make the screen bigger you will need to get rid of the Task pane.

 Click on the Close button in the top right of the Task pane. ————

Only the flyer will now be displayed.

Saving your Publication

Click File on the menu bar and Save. Save it as Disco in an appropriate folder. Publisher will automatically add a file extension .pub to the file name.

You can now close the file without losing your work by selecting File, Close from the menu.

Close Publisher by selecting File, Exit.

Note:

It is a good idea to save your work regularly to prevent losing it by accident. Publisher will automatically prompt you to do this every 15 minutes.

File
Save
Disco.pub

Chapter **2**
Using a Design Template

Now it is time to add some of your own text to the flyer and customise it for your disco.

Opening an existing publication

▶ Load Microsoft Publisher.

▶ Click on Disco in the Open a Publication section of the Task pane. If it is not shown, click More Publications.

Open a publication

P Disco

P Publication1

P brochure

More publications...

Figure 2.1: Opening an existing publication

Opening existing publications is totally simple dudes.

If you cannot see the filename, you can click the down arrow in the **Look In:** box in the Open Publication window. This will bring up a list of folders for you to search.

 Click the Disco.pub file that you created in Chapter 1 and click Open.

Text frames

Publisher organises everything in blocks called 'frames'. These frames can hold text (in text boxes) or pictures (in picture frames).

The template you have been using has set up these frames automatically for you so all you have to do is replace the text in them with your own.

Taking a closer look

Firstly you need to make the flyer bigger so that you can see it more clearly. This is done using the zoom controls on the standard toolbar.

▶ Click on the small down arrow to the right of the Zoom box. ————

▶ Select Page Width. The flyer now fills the width of the page.

'+' and '-' icons for zooming in or out

Figure 2.2: Zooming in on your publication

Tip:

You can also use the '+' and '-' icons next to the zoom control box. These will zoom in or out one step at a time.

Personalising the publication

Now you can begin to add particular details about the school disco that people are going to need to know if they want to come.
To begin with, you are going to change the word 'Party' to the word 'Disco'.

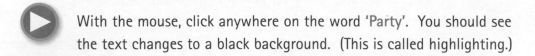 With the mouse, click anywhere on the word 'Party'. You should see the text changes to a black background. (This is called highlighting.)

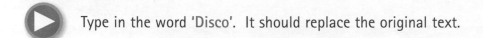 Type in the word 'Disco'. It should replace the original text.

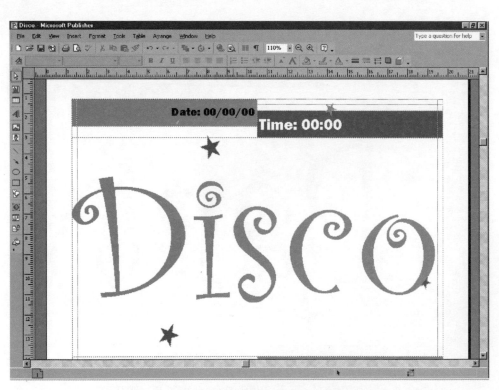

Figure 2.3: Replacing text in a placeholder

Now you are going to do the same for the date and time placeholders.

Click anywhere over the date placeholder at the top of the flyer to highlight it.

 Change the current date to 21 July 2002.

 Now do the same with the time, putting in 19:00 as the time to be there.

The same method can be used to replace all of the remaining text in the other placeholders lower down in the flyer.

If you wish to complete your flyer, look at Figure 2.5 at the end of the chapter for some ideas.

Tip:
A placeholder is text made by Publisher for you to replace with your own text.

Note:
You will notice that the Personal Details you entered in the last chapter are automatically entered for you as the school name and address. These can be changed on the screen in the same way as other text blocks if necessary.

Changing text size

Publisher automatically adjusts the text size so that it fits within the frame of the page but some of it still looks a little big. You will now change the size of some of the text.

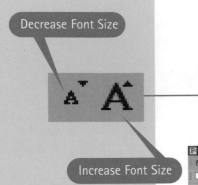

Decrease Font Size

Increase Font Size

▶ First highlight the word Disco by dragging the cursor over the letters.

▶ Click twice on the Decrease Font Size button on the right of the standard toolbar.

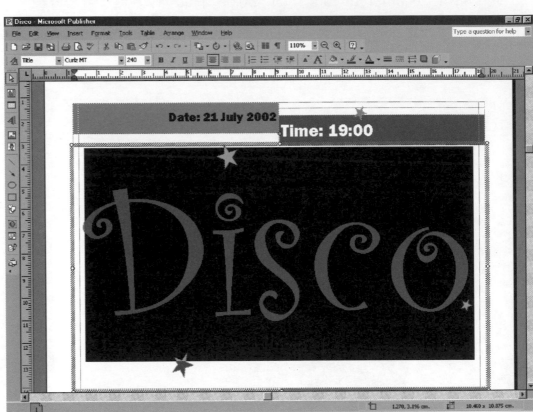

Figure 2.4: Changing the Text Size

Tip:

If you are only changing the text size of one word you do not need to highlight the text. The cursor must just be somewhere in the word.

The text should now look smaller. You can also increase the font size using the Increase Font Size button next to the Decrease Font Size button. These buttons are useful if you only want to make minor adjustments to the size of some text.

Any major adjustments should be made using the drop down Font Size box on the left of the toolbar.

Deleting a placeholder

You are not going to need a logo on this flyer so the placeholder for the logo in the bottom right of the flyer can be removed.

- Move the mouse anywhere over the pyramid graphic. When there is a little moving van next to the pointer, click the left mouse button.

- Press the Delete key. The logo will disappear.
- Save and Close the document.

Figure 2.5: The finished flyer

Chapter 3
Design Sets

A design set is a collection of different sorts of publications that match each other with the same design and colour scheme. For example, a flyer, a calendar, a newsletter and so on.

In this chapter you will begin to develop a school calendar from one of the sets.

> Start by selecting By Design Sets from the drop-down box in the Start from a design section in the Task pane.

> Now select Bars from the Master Sets.

> Click the Bars Calendar.

Tip:
To display the Task pane select View, Task pane.

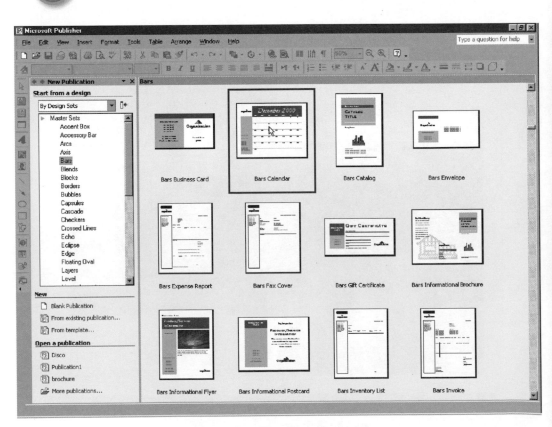

Figure 3.1: The Bars Design Set

 Click Color Schemes in the Task pane.

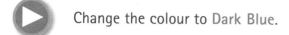 Change the colour to Dark Blue.

 Click Calendar Options.

 Select the Portrait option in the Orientation section.

 With Monthly selected, click the Change date range button.

 Change the Start and End dates to July and click on OK.

Figure 3.2: Changing calendar dates

 Select to include a Schedule of Events.

Your page should now look like the one below. In this screen, the Task pane has been hidden and the page sized to Whole Page.

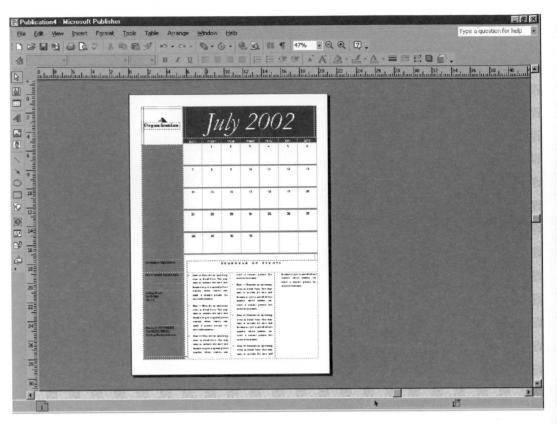

Figure 3.3: The outline for the Bars Calendar design

Now you can begin to add some events to your calendar such as your disco for example. This can be done using text and pictures.

▶ Save your publication as Calendar.

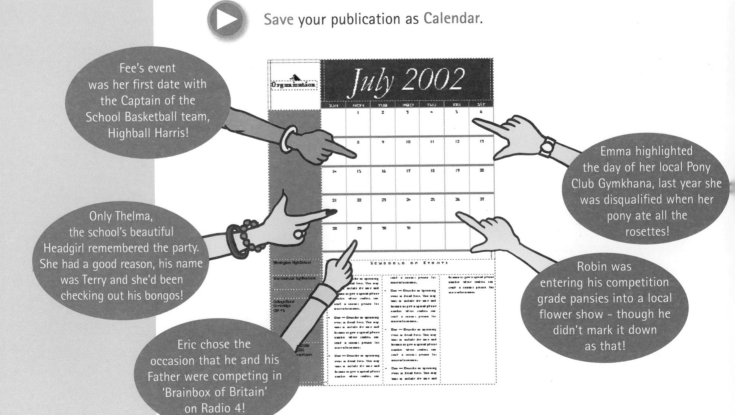

Inserting ClipArt into a publication

To add pictures to your calendar, you must first make sure that the cursor is not on the page.

 To do this click anywhere outside the page borders.

 Now zoom in your calendar to 150% using either the Zoom menu or the Zoom In button.

 Now select Insert, Picture, Clip Art... from the main menu bar. The Task pane should appear.

Figure 3.4: Selecting Clip Art

You are going to add a little picture to describe the disco on the 21st of July.

 In the Search text box, type in music and press Enter.

A selection of clips matching your description should appear in the window.

Select the arrow next to your picture - a menu will appear.

 Click insert to add your clip to the calendar publication.

Note:

If the selection you get is not the same as those shown in the screen below, try choosing a picture of your own or typing in another word in the **Search text** box. You may have a different selection of clips and find something better. In this example, a music note has been used.

Figure 3.5: Inserting Clip Art

Moving and Sizing a graphic

Once you have inserted the picture into your publication you can close the Task pane. You will now need to make the graphic smaller.

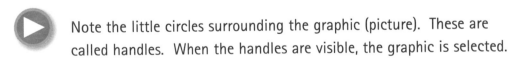 Note the little circles surrounding the graphic (picture). These are called handles. When the handles are visible, the graphic is selected.

▶ Move the mouse pointer over one of the corner handles. You will see the mouse pointer change to say resize.

▶ Drag the handle into the centre of the picture and let go when the picture is small enough to fit inside the area for July 21st on the calendar.

▶ When the mouse pointer turns into a little moving van, you can move the picture.

▶ Move the picture under the 21 in the calendar.

Next you can add a simple word of text under the picture to describe it.

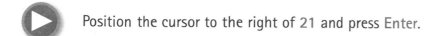 Position the cursor to the right of 21 and press Enter.

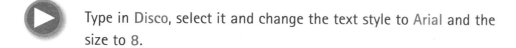 Type in Disco, select it and change the text style to Arial and the size to 8.

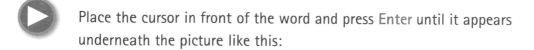 Place the cursor in front of the word and press Enter until it appears underneath the picture like this:

Figure 3.6: End of school disco on the 21st July

You can add other pictures to your calendar for more events such as a sports day, a play or a fundraising event.

Complementing your pictures

You will notice some text frames at the bottom of the page. These are for explaining more about the events in your calendar.

▶ Click the first text frame in the Schedule of Events section and all the text will be highlighted

▶ Delete it by pressing the Delete key.

▶ Write the description given below in the first bullet point.

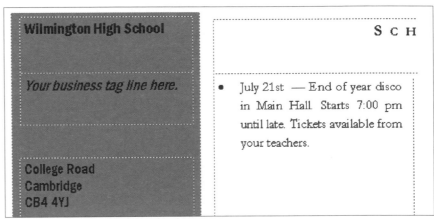

Figure 3.7: Describing events

Publisher leaves plenty of space for more events if you wish to add them in.

Adding to your Design Set

Now you can go on and produce some more publications to match this one by using the same design set.

If you wish the rest of your designs to have the same colour scheme, you need to change this setting in the Personal Information window.

 Select Edit, Personal Information... from the main menu.

 Change the colour scheme from Citrus to Dark Blue.

 Click Update.

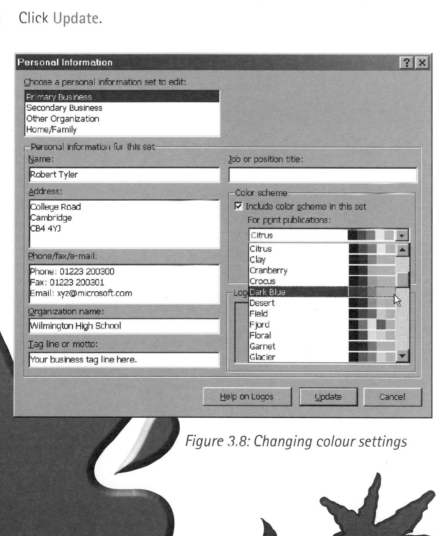

Figure 3.8: Changing colour settings

23

Chapter **4**
Creating a Logo

In this chapter you will learn how to create a logo for your school. You can then use this on any future publication that you may produce.

 First, select File, Open and open your calendar publication called calendar.pub.

The Logo Creation Wizard

To design your new logo you will be using the logo wizard.

 Start by clicking anywhere on the logo at the top of your calendar.

 Zoom in to 200% and scroll the logo into view to see it in more detail.

 You will see a small wand icon appear. Click on this.

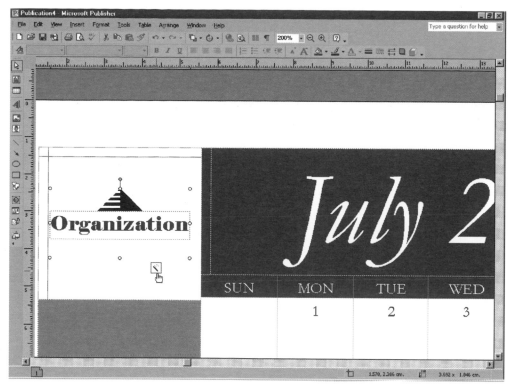

Figure 4.1: Starting the logo wizard

Once you have clicked on the wand icon, the Logo Designs Task pane will appear.

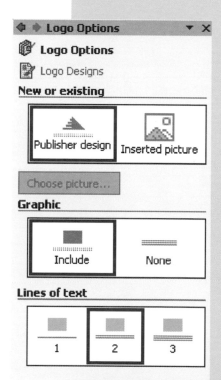

▶ Click on Logo Designs and choose Open Oval from the selection.

▶ Select Logo Options, then 2 under lines of text.

▶ Close the Task pane by clicking the X in the top right corner. Your logo should now look like this:

Figure: 4.2: New logo layout

Now you can enter the name and type of the school into the image and then you will learn how to add your own graphic.

▶ Click on the word Organization and type in Wilmington.

▶ Now type High School in the Name placeholder.

Changing the logo graphic

▶ Double-click the graphic placeholder in the logo. The Insert clip art Task pane will appear.

▶ Search for a clip you would like to see on your logo. I have used the one below but you may have a different selection.

Figure 4.3: The finished logo

Saving your logo

Now that you have created your logo, it is a good idea to save it so that you can put it into other publications straight away without having to recreate it.

 Click File, Save to save the publication as it is so far.

When saving the whole publication, you will be asked if you want to save the logo in your personal information set.

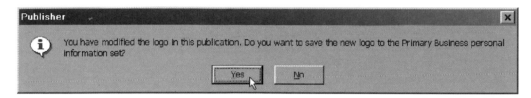

Figure 4.4: Saving your logo

 Click Yes.

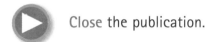 Close the publication.

Using the logo in a new publication

In this section you will create a simple brochure advertising the school. This will include the logo you have just created without the need to redesign it. You will also type in a short piece of text that you will need in the next chapter.

▶ Select File, New from the menu.

▶ Click Brochures in the Start from a design section of the Task pane.

▶ Select the Even Break Fund-raiser Brochure from the Fund-raiser category.

▶ Select Cranberry as the colour scheme and close the Task pane since you do not need to change any of the other options.

You will notice that the logo that you designed previously has automatically been added to this publication because you saved it as part of the personal information set.

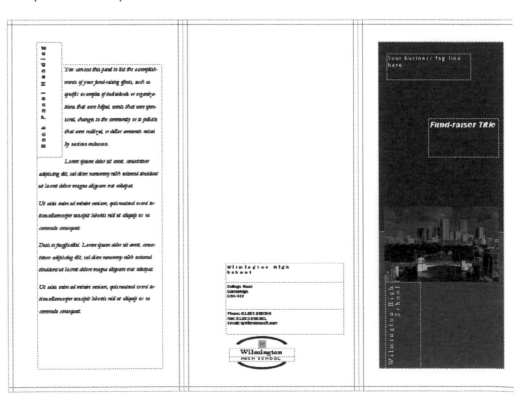

Figure 4.5: School brochure with logo

Importing text from another application

Adding text into a publication can be done in several ways. You have already learned in earlier chapters how to type directly into a text placeholder in Publisher. Now you will see how to import text from another program such as Microsoft Word.

 Load Microsoft Word and begin a new document.

 Type in the following paragraph about the school in 14 point, Times New Roman style.

> Pupils at Wilmington High School benefit from the facilities and staffing of a 'new' school with the very best of our grammar school traditions.
>
> Pupils joining the school in Year 7 are based for the majority of their lessons in the Lower School Centre which provides a stepping stone from primary school to the larger environment of the secondary school.
>
> The purpose-built facilities of the Technology centre provide the basis of all the pupils' Information Technology requirements. Three labs are fully equipped with the latest hardware and software as well as a library of ICT textbooks on basic skills in word processing, desktop publishing and spreadsheets.

 Save the text as Brochure.doc.

In the publishing world, a passage such as this is called a 'story'.

 Highlight the story you have just typed and select Edit, Copy from the main menu.

 Now go back to your brochure in Publisher (by pressing Alt Tab or using the mouse) and click in the paragraph on the left side of the brochure's back cover to select it.

Click on Edit, Paste. Your page should now look like the one below:

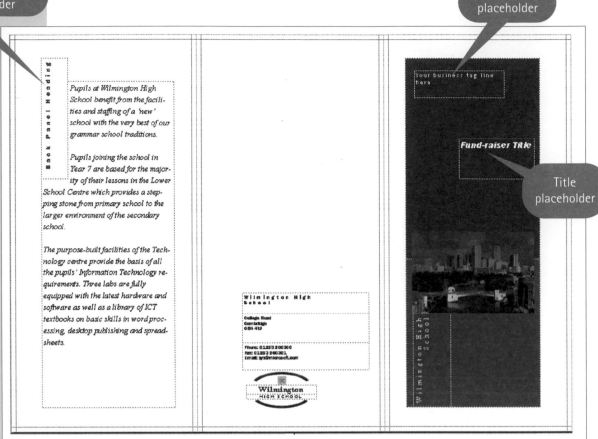

Figure 4.6: Replacing text

 Now replace the text in the Back Panel Heading placeholder (on the left of the paragraph you have just placed) with High School Introduction.

 On the front page, replace the tag line at the top of the page with Traditional values in a modern world, and the Fundraiser Title with the year – 2002 – 2003.

If you would like to finish off this side of the brochure, you can double-click the graphic to insert a picture of your own in the same way as you added the clip art picture to the calendar.

 Save and Close your publication, naming it Brochure.pub.

Chapter 5
Creating a Newsletter

In this chapter you will learn how to create a school newsletter. This will cover some of the really clever features of Publisher.

Starting the newsletter

▶ If Publisher is not already loaded, load it up now. (If it is already loaded, click File, New)

▶ In the Task pane click Newsletters.

▶ Scroll down to the Straight Edge Newsletter design and click the picture.

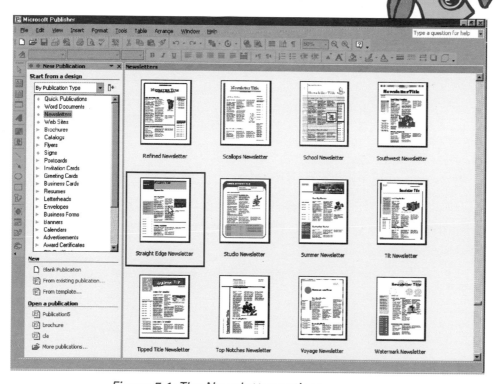

Figure 5.1: The Newsletter options

 Choose Dark Blue as your colour scheme

Click Page Content and choose 2 columns.

Click Newsletter Options and make sure None is selected for customer address.

Select two-sided printing.

Close the Task pane.

Moving between pages

You have been given 4 pages for your publication. To move to another page you just need to click on one of the page icons in the bottom left of the screen.

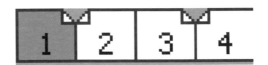

At the moment you are on page 1. Click on the Page 4 icon to move to page 4.

Whilst creating his own newsletter Robin's exuberant keyboard technique and "Quiet, Maestro at work" signs were starting to earn him a bit of a reputation.

Your page should look like this:

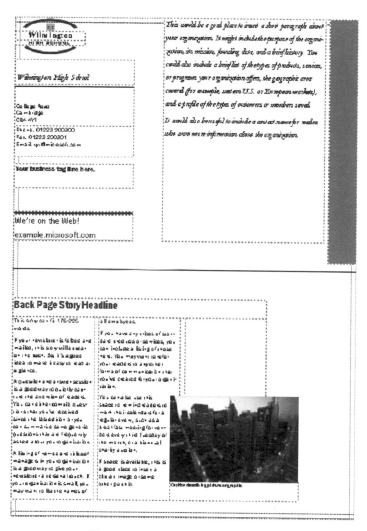

Figure 5.2: The back page

Inserting another Personal Information Set component

At the top of the 4th page you will see that Publisher has automatically added the logo you designed in the previous chapter. Suppose you want to add another logo to the front page.

Click the Page 1 icon to move back to the first page.

Click the Insert menu.

Now click Personal Information.

Click on Logo.

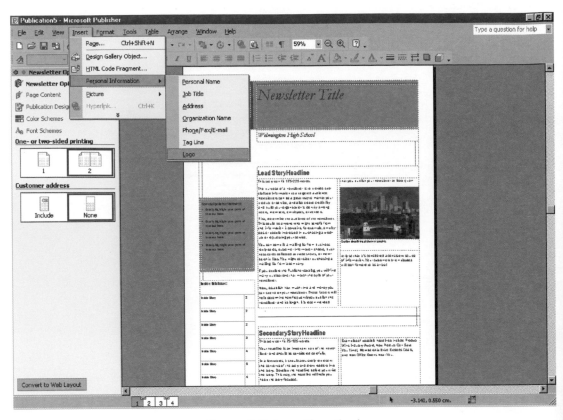

Figure 5.3: Inserting the logo

A copy of your logo will appear on the page.

 Position the mouse over the logo until it changes into a moving van icon and move it to the top right corner of the newsletter.

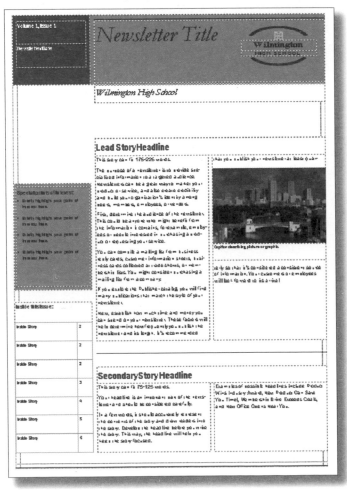

Figure 5.4

Make the logo slightly bigger to fill the space so that it appears as in figure 5.4 on the previous page.

 Save your publication as Newsletter.pub.

Copying a story from another publication

So far you have seen how to add text directly into Publisher and how to copy from Microsoft Word. You can also copy it from a different publication in Publisher.

 Open the Brochure publication that you created in chapter 4.

 Position the cursor in the back page story that you wrote and select Edit, Select All from the menu.

 Now, in the same way as you did in Microsoft Word, select Edit, Copy from the menu and reopen the Newsletter publication.

Although this text is not particularly suitable for a newsletter, it is good for showing you how Microsoft Publisher works with larger stories.

 Click on the text placeholder for the lead story under the Lead Story Headline.

 Select Edit, Paste from the menu.

You should now see your story on the front page of your newsletter.

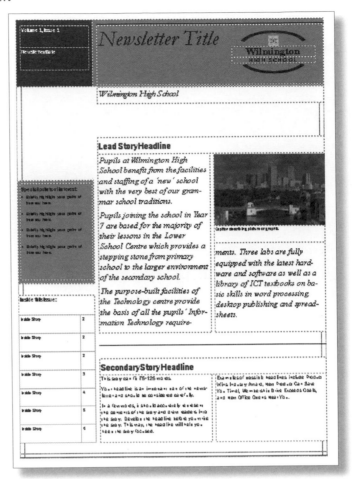

Figure 5.5: The newsletter front page

Now, supposing your story was too big to fit in the space provided?

 Move your cursor to the end of the story and select **Edit, Paste** again from the menu. This will add a copy of the story on the end of the original to make it seem longer.

Because there is too much text to fit in the frame, Publisher will display a message asking if you would like to use autoflow.

 Click **No**.

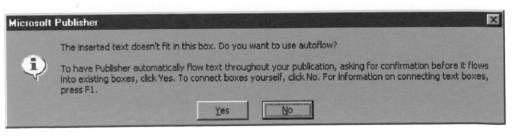

Figure 5.6

The text that you cannot see is stored in an 'Overflow' area, indicated by this icon at the end of the story. When this happens you can either increase the size of the current frame, decrease the size of the text or continue the story in another frame inside the newsletter to leave room for a different story at the bottom of the front page.

 Select Edit, Select All and change the text size to 12.

 Change the Font Style to Arial.

 Save the publication as Newsletter.pub.

Making the text smaller had little effect because there was a lot of overflow. You can now try continuing the story on another page.

Connecting frames

Now you will see how to put the overflow text into another frame.

 First move to the top inside story on page 2.

 Highlight the story and press Delete to remove all the contents of the placeholder.

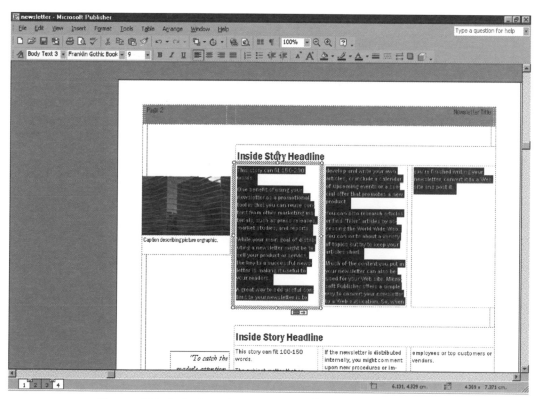

Figure 5.7: Deleting the contents of a placeholder

 Go back to page 1 and select View, Toolbars, Connect Frames from the menu.

The text on page 1 is in two separate, connected frames.

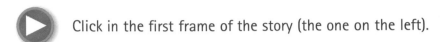 Click in the first frame of the story (the one on the left).

 Move to the next frame by clicking the Go To Next Text Box button on the toolbar.

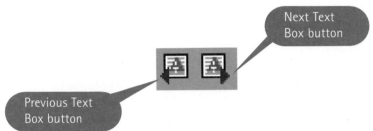

Next Text Box button

Previous Text Box button

You will see the second frame selected. Now the Go To Next Text Box button will be greyed out, because there are no more frames containing part of this story.

Tip:
You have to be in the last frame before placing any overflow text.

 Now click on the Create Text Box Link button on the toolbar.

 You will see the mouse pointer turn into a jug of letters. Move to the story on page 2.

 Hold the mouse over the empty frame and when the mouse pointer turns into a pouring jug of letters, click the mouse to pour them out into the placeholder.

You should now see the remainder of your story appear in the frame on page 2.

Continued on next page...

Now all you need to do is to tell your reader where to look for the rest of the story if they have finished reading the beginning of it.

 Go to the story on page 1.

 Click the mouse within the text in the second frame of the first page.

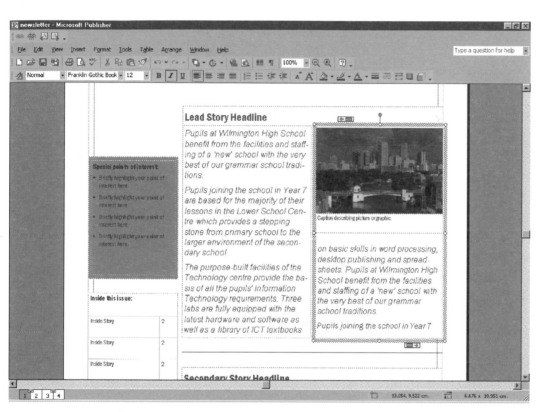

Figure 5.8: The second text frame is selected

The text overflow took Eric a bit by surprise!

 Now right-click the text box and click **Format Text Box**.

 Click the **Text Box** tab and check the **Include "Continued on page..."** box. Click **OK**.

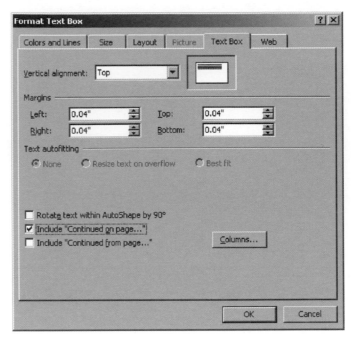

Figure 5.9: Adding "Continued on" lines

Now you should have successfully added a line telling readers to go to page 2 for more of the story.

You can also add another line at the beginning of the second half of the story on page 2 saying "Continued from page 1".

Click the **Go To Next Frame** button on the toolbar.

Now right-click and select **Format Text Box**, click the **Text Box** tab and check the **Include "Continued from page..."** box. Click **OK**.

Save and **Close** the publication.

Chapter **6**
Working without Templates

In this chapter you will design your own CD inlay card. Publisher does not have a template for this so you will learn how to make it from scratch.

Creating a blank publication

▶ First click File, New from the main menu.

▶ In the Start from a design section of the Task pane select By Blank Publications from the drop-down box.

▶ Click Book Fold.

▶ You will be asked if you want to automatically add 3 extra pages. Click No.

The guys finally found out that working with templates had its creative drawbacks.

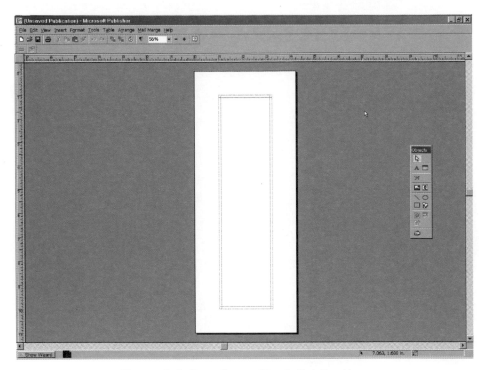

Figure 6.1: Creating a Blank Publication

Changing the page size

You will notice that the shape of the page is not the same as a CD inlay card so this is the next thing to change.

▶ Click File, Page Setup... from the Main Menu.

▶ Change the Width measurement to 9.5" and the Height to 4.7".

▶ Set the Orientation to Landscape and click OK as shown below:

Tip:

You can change the measurement units by selecting Tools, Options and clicking the General tab.

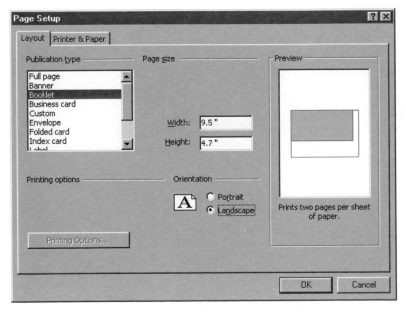

Figure 6.2: Changing the page sizes

Changing page margins

You will notice that there are several pink and blue lines already on the page. These guides are called margins. They are used either to give the page a white border to naturally make it stand out or to help you lay out a page design.

You do not want any margins in your CD cover design.

▶ From the Main Menu, click Arrange, Layout Guides...

▶ Change all of the Margin Guides to 0".

▶ You will need 2 Columns. (One for each side of the cover).

▶ Deselect 'Create Two Master Pages with Mirrored Guides'.

▶ Click OK. twice.

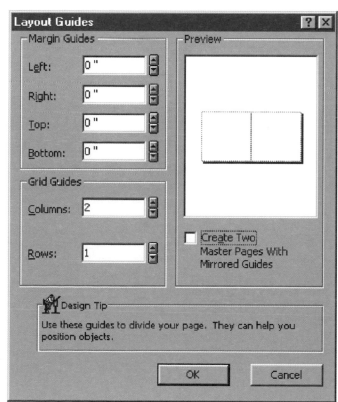

Figure 6.3: Changing the margins

▶ Now Save your template. Call it CD Cover.pub.

Inserting a picture

This tutorial has used a picture from the Microsoft Online Clip Art collection. You may not have the same picture but you can use a photograph of your own.

Click the Picture Frame Tool on the Objects toolbar.

Click and drag a frame over the entire right-hand half of the page. Your page should now have handles around the right page.

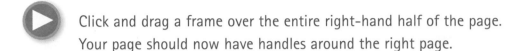

Figure 6.4: Inserting a picture frame

You will now see a window in which you can search for a picture that you want. This exercise will use the one shown below:

Figure 6.5: Searching for a picture

Click Insert to put the picture into your publication.

Moving and sizing an image

Once you have inserted the image, you will need to make it bigger to fit the front cover better.

 Move the picture so that it is at the edge of the right hand page.

 Now drag the top right handle away from the picture until it is the same width as the frame. (Don't worry about the height at this point.)

Figure 6.6: Sizing an image

 Now Move the picture down a little so that the top and bottom hang off the page.

Cropping an image

When you have moved the picture into position, you will need to cut off the bits that don't fit on the page. This is called 'cropping'.

▶ Click anywhere on the picture once if it is not already selected.

▶ Make sure the Picture toolbar is visible.

▶ Now click the Crop Picture button.

▶ Position the mouse over the top-centre handle. The pointer should turn into 2 pairs of scissors.

▶ Now drag the top of the picture down until it is level with the top edge of the page.

▶ Now do the same to the bottom of the picture.

Figure 6.7: Cropping an image

Adding a text frame

Now you can add something to the back page of the cover.
You may just like to keep it simple for now so add your name to
the design.

▶ Click the Text Box Tool.

▶ Now click and drag a small rectangle for your name at the bottom of
the left page.

▶ Type Cover design by 'YOUR NAME'

▶ Select the text and Centre it.

▶ Use the Increase Font Size button make your name bigger.

▶ With the text still selected, click the arrow next to the Font Color
button and click More Colors...

▶ Select a dark blue shade and click OK.

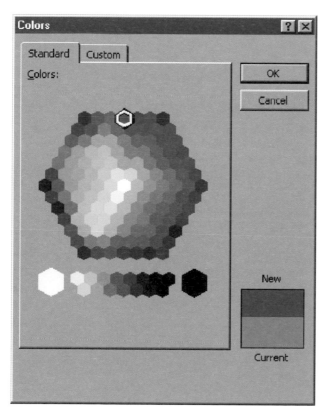

Figure 6.8: Selecting colour shades

▶ Click the arrow next to the Fill Color button.

▶ Select No Fill. This will make the background transparent – the effects of this you will notice later.

▶ Your cover should look like the one shown below.

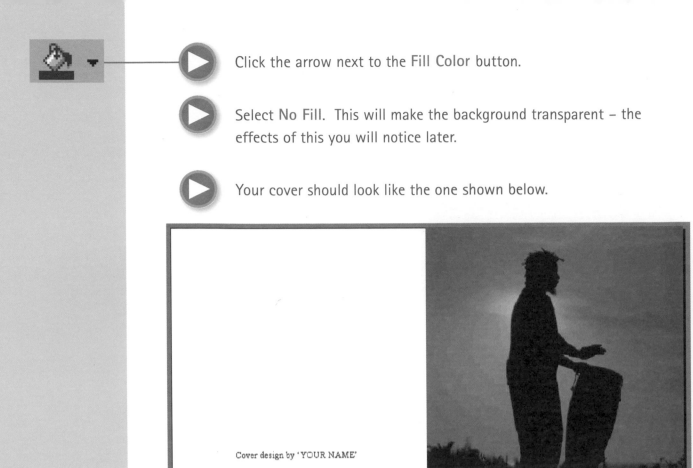

Cover design by 'YOUR NAME'

Figure 6.9: Adding a Text Frame

▶ Save your work to prevent losing your efforts so far.

Adding blocks of colour

Adding areas of colour is achieved using different coloured shapes. You are going to make the back of the cover orange to match the sky in the photo.

▶ Click the Rectangle Tool.

▶ Click and drag a rectangle over the entire page.

▶ Now (with the rectangle selected) click the arrow next to the Fill Color button.

▶ Choose More Fill Colors..., click the Standard tab and select an orange shade.

▶ Click OK.

Order – In front or behind?

You will notice that the orange has covered up everything else.
To solve this problem, you need to make the orange a background.

 Select the orange rectangle.

 Click the arrow next to the Order button and select Send to Back. ———

If you want to bring something to the front you can select Bring
To Front.

You will also notice that the box containing your name is transparent. This is because you chose No Fill Color.

Adding fancy lettering

Microsoft Publisher and Word both have something called WordArt. This allows you to create more interesting text than ordinary-looking letters.

 Click the Insert WordArt button.

 Choose the top-left style and click OK.

WordArt will automatically give you a box to type your text into.

 Type Bongo and click OK.

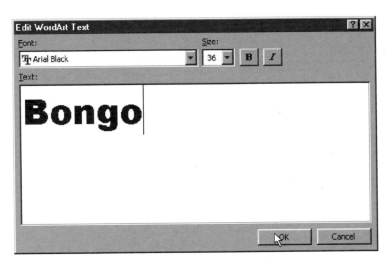

Figure 6.10: Inserting WordArt

Whilst lacking in finesse or any sense of rhythm, Terry's Bongo playing made up for it with awesome, deaf-defying volume!

50

Special Effects

Now it is time to add some special effects...

Using the Wordart toolbar shown below, add the following effects to the text.

▶ Choose the Format Wordart button on the Wordart toolbar.

▶ Change the line colour to orange and click OK.

▶ Click the Edit Text button on the Wordart toolbar.

▶ Change the Font to Times New Roman, and click OK.

▶ Click away from the text.

Figure 6.11: WordArt text

Your text should look something like the picture above.
There are also many, many other effects that you can create such as rotating and shadowing text. Try these effects out on some more WordArt text of your own. The easiest way to learn new things is to experiment.

Add some more WordArt Text Frames like in the picture below.
Hint: Just change the size and shading for these examples.

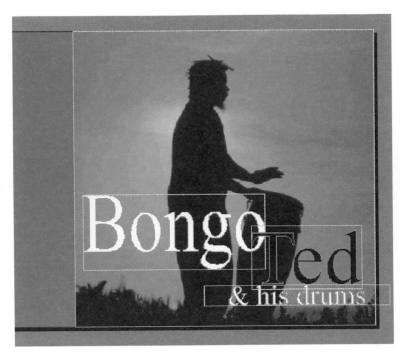

Figure 6.12: More WordArt

Whilst striving to improve his art, Terry became one of the least popular members of the local community.

Grouping objects

You can group all of the WordArt Text Frames. This means that they will all move when you move one and behave as if they were all one object.

 Hold down the Shift key and click on each frame, one at a time.

You will notice a little grey and black puzzle icon appearing. This is the **Group Objects** button.

 Click the **Group Objects** button. The puzzle pieces will join to become the **Ungroup Objects** button.

Figure 6.13: The finished cover

Chapter 7

A Professional Look

In this chapter you will continue working on your CD cover. This time though, you will be finishing the inside of it.

You will add a track list and some more special effects with text and colours.

Inserting a new page

To begin, you will need to insert a new page.

 Click Insert, Page... from the Main Menu.

 Choose to insert 1 new page After current page.

Figure 7.1: The Insert Page dialogue box

 Click OK.

You will again be asked (as you were in chapter 6) if you want extra pages. Click NO.

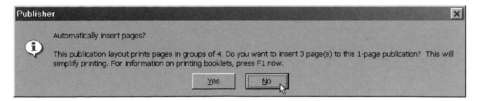

Figure 7.2: Automatically insert pages ?

You will see your new page. (Note the page 2 icon in the bottom left of the screen is highlighted.)

Creating a Table

To add the track listing you are going to create a simple table showing the track number, title and length.

 Click the Insert Table button on the toolbar.

 Click and drag a small rectangle on the right hand side of the page.

 The Table window will appear. Choose 4 Rows with 3 Columns and select the List with Title 2 format as shown below:

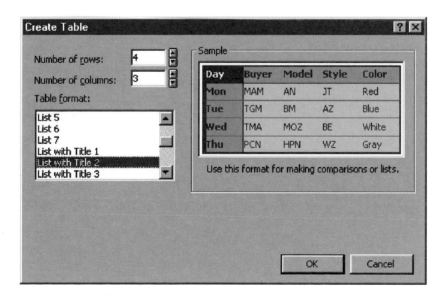

Figure 7.3: The Create Table window

 Click OK.

You should now see the empty table on your page.

Click in each box to enter text. Fill in the table with the details given in the picture below:

Track Number	Title	Length
1	Drummerman	4.17
2	Rain Dance	6.57
3	Jungle Beat	3.44

Figure 7.4: The finished table

 Highlight all the cells and increase the Font Size to 12.

Creating a Drop Cap

This section is going to show you how to create a piece of text where the first letter of the paragraph is bigger than the rest of the text. This is called a Drop Cap.

  Click the Text Box button.

 Click and drag a large rectangle on the left hand side of the page.

 Type the text shown in the picture below:

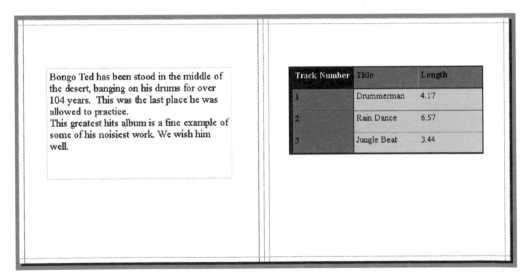

Figure 7.5: The page so far...

 Highlight the text and increase the Font Size to 16.

Now you are ready to add the drop cap.

 Highlight the first paragraph in the Text Frame and click on Format, Drop Cap... from the Main Menu.

 Choose the style shown below and click on Apply, then OK.

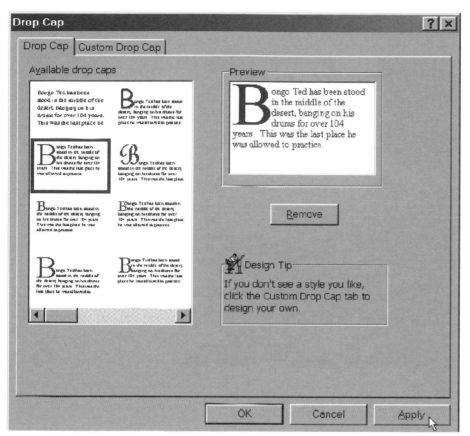

Figure 7.6: Selecting a Drop Cap style

 Enlarge the Text Frame if you need to.

Your page should look like the page shown below:

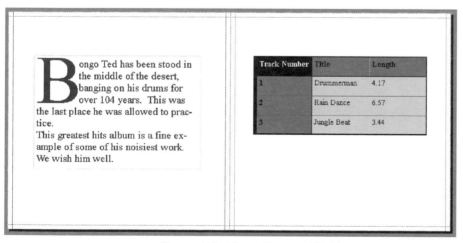

Figure 7.7: Drop Cap and Table

 Remember to save your work regularly. Save your work now.

Making a Border

You may think that the Text Frame needs a border. To add one follow the next few steps.

 Click on the Text Frame once to highlight it.

 Now click on the Line/Border Style button.

Select the 1st line option on the menu after 'No Line'.

Shading

Now it is time to liven up the background of your inside cover. You are going to give it a Sunset effect to match the picture on the front.

 Click the Rectangle Tool and click and drag a rectangle that covers the entire page.

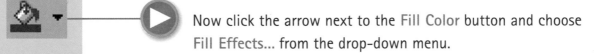 Now click the arrow next to the Fill Color button and choose Fill Effects... from the drop-down menu.

 Click the Gradient tab.

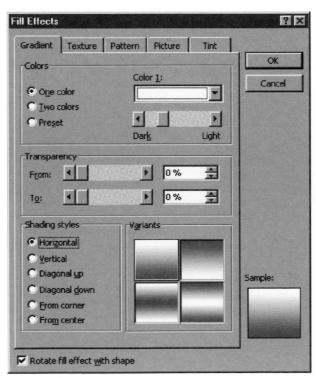

Figure 7.8: Creating a Fill Effect

▶ Now click Two Colors and click More Colors... in the Color 1 drop-down box.

▶ Click the Standard tab and choose an Orange shade.

▶ Click OK.

▶ Now do the same to Color 2. Change it to a lighter Orange shade and click OK.

▶ In the Variants section select the top-left option with a horizontal shading style and click OK.

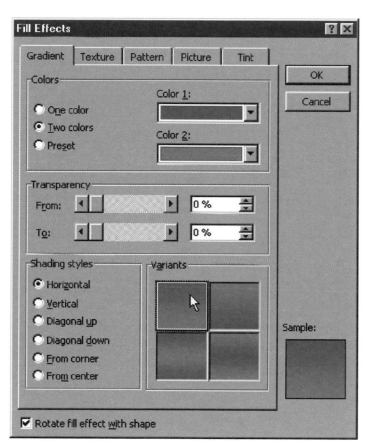

Figure 7.9: The sunset effect

You will now see your results. Unfortunately, the table and text is covered up so you need to send the background rectangle to the back.

With the rectangle highlighted click the arrow next to the Order button on the standard toolbar and select Send to back.

As a finishing touch, remove the background fill from the text frame. Highlight the frame and click on the Fill Color arrow. Select No Fill.

Now Save your work.

Your finished inside cover should look like the one below:

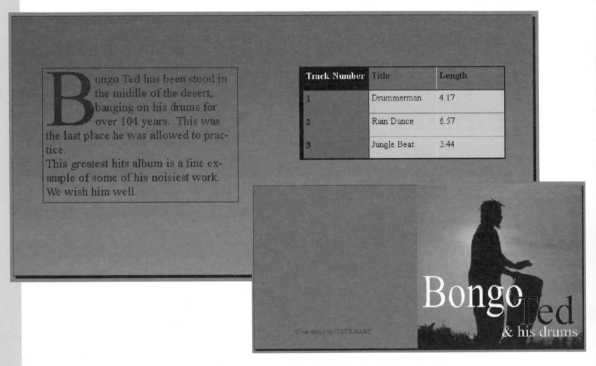

Figure 7.10: The finished publication!

He's the living legend of the 'Bingo - Bango - Bongo - Beat, The one and only...

...Bongo Ted!

Chapter 8
Finishing Off

Brightening things up

As you will now have learned, there are many tools in Publisher such as clip art, pictures and word art that can you help you liven up a publication.

It is always good to include a few colourful images to ease the reader into it and to complement what you are saying. No one wants to stare at a boring block of black and white text!

White Space

In the publishing world, 'white space' is an area of the page where there is nothing printed. It is these areas that usually need livening up.

Keep it simple

One of the most important things to remember is not to clutter up your page.

It is easy to get carried away when livening up a page especially when it is to advertise something.

Sometimes if you add too many clever graphics or pictures, people end up paying more attention to them than to the content of the publication itself.

Boundaries and Guides

Publisher adds boundary lines to help you see the different areas of the page when you are designing it.

Sometimes it is helpful to see your work as it will look when it is printed.

 To remove the guidelines: click on View, and uncheck the Boundaries and Guides option.

 To replace the guidelines: click on View, and check the Boundaries and Guides option.

  To preview how a single page will look on paper, click the Print Preview button.

 Click Close to return to the main Publisher window.

Proofreading

When you have finished your publication, it is always a good idea to read it through yourself to find any mistakes that you may have missed. This is called proofreading.

A spellchecker is a good way to start off but this cannot find errors in the content of what you are saying or find missing words!

 To do this click Tools, Spelling, Spelling from the Main Menu.

One of the most important tips in proofreading is to print it out first.

Another good way to find errors is to get someone else to proofread it. Often people find it easier to spot other people's mistakes than their own. Several people will have read this book before it was first printed so hopefully you won't find any misstakes in it...

It is very hard to spot all of your mistakes when your publication is still on the computer screen.

Printing it out

Once you have finished, you will want to print your work.

 To do this click File, Print on the menu.

It is likely that you will have to print it out more than once before you get it all right.

Bongo Ted was well pleased with his new CD cover.
"Bongotastic" he said, and whilst everyone enjoyed a good chat with him,
Terry was dumbstruck at the sight of his hero and
could only manage a little dribble.

Index